What's the difference be and herpes?

You get mono by snatching a kiss.

●

What's brown and sits on a piano bench?

Beethoven's first movement.

●

What do you call a child raised in a house of ill repute?

A brothel sprout.

●

Did you hear what happened to the man who had sex with his canary?

He got twerpies, and the worst thing is that it's untweetable.

●

What's the difference between an elephant and an Italian grandmother?

Twenty pounds and a black dress.

●

How can you separate the men from the boys in a gay bar?

With a crowbar.

**TURN THE PAGE FOR MORE OUTRAGEOUSLY OFFENSIVE JOKES!**

# OUTRAGEOUSLY OFFENSIVE JOKES

## Maude Thickett

ARROW BOOKS

Arrow Books Limited
17-21 Conway Street, London W1P 6JD

An imprint of the Hutchinson Publishing Group

London Melbourne Sydney Auckland
Johannesburg and agencies throughout
the world

First published in Great Britain 1984
Reprinted 1985 (twice)

Compiled and adapted from
*Outrageously Offensive Jokes*
and
*Outrageously Offensive Jokes II*
by Maude Thickett,
both originally published in the USA by Pocket Books

© 1983 by Pocket Books, a division of Simon & Schuster, Inc.

This book is sold subject to the condition that it
shall not, by way of trade or otherwise, be lent,
resold, hired out, or otherwise circulated without
the publisher's prior consent in any form of
binding or cover other than that in which it is
published and without a similar condition
including this condition being imposed on the
subsequent purchaser

Set in Lectura type
by Photobooks (Bristol) Ltd

Printed and bound in Great Britain by
Anchor Brendon Limited, Tiptree, Essex

ISBN 0 09 934950 7

This book is a work of fiction. Names,
characters, places and incidents are either the
product of the author's imagination or are used
fictitiously. Any resemblance to actual events or
locales or persons, living or dead, is entirely
coincidental.

*For Joseph and Rosemarie
and their 'son' Baron*

# Acknowledgements

I would like to thank the many people who have contributed to the making of this book. Many will remain nameless to protect their reputations, but there are a few brave souls who don't give a damn. Although not completely identified, they are as follows:

Many thanks to Stuart M., Jim 7., Kate F., Scott A., Debbie S., Brian B., Vinnie V., Sandy R., Trish B., Yolanda I., Mike P., and Robin S.

My thanks also go to the gang at 'the show', along with Dom and Grace G., Jim and Rose C., and Jimmy 'the weed' C., and my deepest gratitude to Uncle Dutch – he had a million of 'em.

# Contents

# Celebrities

How can you identify Dolly Parton's kids at a party?

They're the ones with stretch marks around their mouths.

●

What do you get when you cross a black man with Bo Derek?

The ten of spades.

●

President Reagan was flying back to the U.S. after special talks with Cuban leaders. As his helicopter passed over the Florida Everglades, he spotted two white men in a speedboat, dragging a black man behind them on a rope.

Reagan asked the pilot to bring the chopper down alongside the boat. Once in hearing range, Reagan turned on the microphone and yelled, 'I sure do think it's wonderful of you two boys to take a black man water-skiing. It's refreshing to see that there isn't any prejudice in Florida.'

As the helicopter flew off, one of the boaters turned to the other and said, 'He may be president of the whole fucking country, but he sure don't know shit about huntin' alligator.'

●

What's black and white and has three eyes?

Sammy Davis Jr. and his ex-wife.

•

A woman walks into a tattoo parlour.

'Do you do custom work?' she asks the artist.

'Why of course!'

'Good. I'd like a portrait of Robert Redford on the inside of my right thigh, and a portrait of Paul Newman on the inside of my left thigh.'

'No problem,' says the artist. 'Strip from the waist down and get up on the table.'

After two hours of hard work, the artist finishes. The woman sits up and examines the tattoos.

'That doesn't look like them!' she complains loudly.

'Oh yes it does,' the artist says indignantly, 'and I can prove it.' With that, he runs out of the shop and grabs the first man off the street he can find; it happens to be the town drunk.

'Well, what do you think?' the woman asks, spreading her legs. 'Do you know who these men are?'

The drunk studies the tattoos for a couple of minutes and says. 'I'm not sure who the guys on either side are, but the fellow in the middle is definitely Willie Nelson!'

•

What part of Popeye never rusts?

The part he puts in Olive Oyl.

•

What do Linda Lovelace and the Bermuda Triangle have in common?

They both swallow seamen.

•

What's Margaret Thatcher's favourite song?

Don't Falk with me, Argentina.

•

Why does Nancy Reagan always climb on top?

Because Ronnie can only fuck-up.

●

Do you know what happened when the last pope died?

Another one just poped up.

●

What do a male prostitute and the Pink Panther have in common?

They're both peter sellers.

●

What do you get when you cross Billie Jean King with Bo Derek?

A DC 10.

●

Superman is on his way to a large reunion of superheroes being held in Miami Beach. He arrives two hours late, his clothes are a mess and he has definitely been in a fight. As he approaches his table, his good friend Batman yells, 'Hey Man Of Steel, what happened to you?'

'Well, this is gonna sound crazy but I was zipping along the coastline, making great time, when suddenly I look down and there lying on the beach is Wonder Woman - naked!'

'Wow!' says Robin, 'What did you do?'

'What do you think I did, kid?' Her legs were spread, so I figured I was in like Flynn. I dived like an eagle!'

'Boy, I bet she was surprised,' says The Hulk.

Superman smiled weakly and said, 'Yeah, but not as much as the Invisible Man was.'

●

# Maladies

Did you hear about the guy who lost his whole left side in an accident?

He's all right.

•

How did herpes leave the hospital?

On crotches.

•

The doctor went into his patient's room and said, 'I've got some good news and some bad news. Which do you want to hear first?'

'The bad news,' said the frightened patient.

'During your hernia operation the resident's knife slipped, and cut off your penis.'

'My God! Then what's the good news?'

'It wasn't malignant.'

•

How did the leper stop the card game?

He threw his hand in.

•

What's the hardest part of a vegetable to eat?

The wheelchair.

•

How did Captain Hook meet his death?

Crotch itch.

●

An old man went to the doctor.

'Doctor, you've got to help me. Every morning at six o'clock I have to pass water and move my bowels.'

'So what's wrong with that?'

'You don't understand! I don't get up until nine o'clock!'

●

The captain went to his sergeant and said, 'We need a very special man for a very dangerous mission. He must be extraordinarily brave, highly dependable, and have nerves of steel. Think about it tonight; we can talk in the morning about who you feel is the right man for the job.'

'I don't need the time, sir,' the sergeant said. 'I already know that Private Jones is our man.'

'What makes you so sure?'

'Because last week while we were showing the men the training film on VD, he ate strawberry shortcake through the whole damn movie.'

●

What's the difference between mononucleosis and herpes?

You get mono by snatching a kiss.

●

Did you hear what happened to the man who had sex with his canary?

He got twerpies, and the worst thing is that it's untweetable.

●

Mr. Stern hadn't been feeling very well lately, so his loving wife made an appointment for him with their family doctor. She asked the doctor to let her know immediately if the prognosis was unfavourable; she would break the news to her husband gently.

Later that day, the doctor phoned. It was very bad; as a matter of fact it was much worse than he originally thought – her husband had less than twenty-four hours to live. The only blessing was that when he went, it would be quick and painless.

Mrs. Stern decided that this last night would be the most wonderful night of her husband's life. She prepared his favourite meal and met him at the door with his favourite cocktail in hand. After an exquisite meal, they retired to the darkened bedroom for after-dinner drinks. Mrs. Stern put on her sexiest nightgown and perfume and approached her husband. 'Whatever you want to do, whatever fantasies you have, tonight is the night to fulfil them.'

They made wild, passionate love. 'That was great,' said Mr. Stern. 'Let's do it again.' So they did, and he said, 'That was even better. Let's do it again!'

'That's easy for you to say,' said his wife. 'You don't have to get up in the morning.'

●

Did you hear about the queer deaf-mute?

Neither did he.

●

What happened when the butcher backed into his meat grinder?

He got a little behind in his orders.

●

A woman is undressing in front of her husband on their wedding night. He notices that the nipple of her left breast is located on the side of the breast. Then he sees that her navel is off-centre, almost all the way over on her left hip. Unable to hide his surprise and revulsion, he exclaims, 'Boy, are you built strange!'

Naturally offended, his bride lifts her arm, points to her armpit and says, 'Yeah? Well you can kiss my ass!'

●

What's the difference between love and herpes?

Herpes is forever.

●

Ask a leper for an inch and he'll give you a foot.

●

Why did they have to call off the lepers' hockey game?

There was a face off in the corner.

●

Did you hear about the man who had five pricks?

His pants fit him like a glove.

●

The Hunchback of Notre Dame wanted to go on vacation. He asked the bishop for some time off.

'But who will ring the bell?' asked the bishop.

'I don't know,' replied Quasimodo. 'All I know is that I really need a vacation. Why don't you find a temporary replacement?'

So the bishop put up a help wanted sign outside the cathedral. No one, it seemed, was interested in ringing the bell for a week or two while Quasimodo was on vacation. On the day before Quasimodo was due to leave for the south of France, two men walked into the bishop's office. They were identical except for the fact that one of the men had no arms.

'I'd like to ring the bell while Quasimodo is on vacation,' said the man with arms. 'My brother here will be taking over for me on Sundays; I go to church at Chartres.'

The bishop was desperate for a replacement so he agreed to let the man give it a try. He took the brothers to the top of the bell tower. The first brother grabbed the rope and pulled it hard. Off went the bell - a beautiful, clear ring. Excited, the man ran over to embrace his brother. 'We've got the job!' he yelled. In his excitement, however, the man bumped the guard rail which, being old, gave way. The bishop heard a sickening thud as the man hit the ground.

'Well, I guess I'd better give it a try,' said the armless brother.

'Be serious,' said the bishop. 'You can't possibly ring that bell.'

'Listen, your Holiness. You should at least give me a chance. Look at it this way; it's your last chance to find a replacement for Quasimodo.'

The bishop agreed reluctantly, and the armless man took a good running start, flinging himself at the famous bell. He hit it face first, and the huge bell swung loudly. Unfortunately, the force of the swinging bell knocked the man off the top of the bell tower. The bishop heard another thud, and ran to get a doctor.

When the doctor arrived, he did a quick examination of both men. He pronounced the first man dead, and the armless man alive, but unconscious.

'Who is this man?' asked the doctor, pointing to the armless man.

'I don't know,' said the bishop, 'but his face sure rings a bell.'

'And who's the other guy?' the doctor queried.

'Don't know that either,' replied the bishop. 'But he's a dead ringer for his brother.'

●

What do you get when you sit on a stereo?

Steroids.

●

What do promiscuous angels get?

Harpies!

•

A man ran into his doctor's office one day, all excited. The nurse asked him what was wrong.

'I have something wrong with my pecker,' replied the man.

The nurse told the man he couldn't enter the office yelling things about his private parts, and requested that he go outside, enter the office again, and say he had something wrong with, say, his ear.

The patient went outside and returned. 'I have something wrong with my ear.'

'And what exactly is wrong with your ear?' asked the nurse.

'I can't piss out of it,' came the man's reply.

•

If shrimps come over on shrimp boats, where do crabs come from?

The captain's dinghy.

•

A young woman arrives in the United States fresh off a ship from France. Her first stop is a drug store where she asks the druggist for some 'medication for bugs in the bush'. Getting her drift, the druggist gives her the strongest remedy he has for the crabs.

A couple of weeks go by and the French woman and the druggist meet on the street outside the store. He asks, with a sly smile, whether the bugs in the bush have gone.

She replies, 'Ah, monsieur, the bugs, they are gone, the bush, it is gone, and so, monsieur, is Pierre's moustache!'

•

What do you call a legless man water-skiing?

Skip.

●

A man with a draining boil at the crack of his ass goes to a doctor to seek help. The doctor asks the man to drop his pants, so he can see the problem.

The doctor says, 'That is the most disgusting thing I have ever seen. You are dripping pus and blood over everything. Please leave at once!'

In anger, the man leaves. He goes to a second doctor, but he, too, refuses to treat him.

Upon arriving at a third doctor's office, claiming he has an emergency case, the doctor looks at this draining boil, and says that he also is unable to help the man, but a guy called Felix Pussucker is the one to see. The doctor tells the man that Felix can be found down at the shipyards.

After questioning several dockworkers, he finds Felix, who asks him to drop his pants, so that he can see the problem.

'All right, bend over and spread your cheeks,' says Felix, as he proceeds to place his mouth on the man's boil and suck out the pus. Felix is enjoying it immensely, as pus and blood run down his chin. In the middle of this, the man produces a huge fart, right in Felix's face.

Felix suddenly removes his face from the man's ass, turns him around and, in obvious annoyance, says, 'You know, it's guys like you that really make this job disgusting!'

●

The doctor in our town is so bad that he treated a guy for yellow jaundice for five years before he realized the man was Chinese.

●

Why do lepers like potato chips?

Because they can use the back of each other's heads as dips.

A man who is having gas problems explains to his doctor that every time he farts it sounds like 'HONDA'.

The doctor does an examination and finds nothing wrong with the man. As a last resort he looks into his patient's mouth and finally spots the problem.

'I'm sorry, you'll have to go to a dentist for your problem.'

So the man goes to see his dentist. After a quick examination the dentist announces he has an abcess. 'No problem, I'll have you fit and without your embarrassing problem in a jiffy,' said the dentist.

Sure enough, the man's problem disappears and he no longer makes farts that sound like 'HONDA'.

The next week the man calls up the dentist and thanks him for all he's done for him. But before he hangs up he asks the dentist how he knew his problem was caused by his abcess.

The dentist replied, 'It's easy. Everyone knows abcess makes the farts go honda!'

# Various Villainies

Why do female paratroopers wear jockstraps?

So they don't whistle on the way down.

●

Susan was standing on a street corner when a man stopped and said, 'Excuse me, miss, but did you know that you have a tampon hanging out of your mouth?' 'Oh my God,' she said. 'What did I do with my cigarette?'

●

Did you hear what happened to the fly on the toilet seat?

He got pissed off.

●

Miss White asked her class to use the word 'definitely' in a sentence.

Little Lucy raised her hand. 'The sky is definitely blue.'

'That was a very good answer, dear, but the sky is sometimes pink, or grey, too. "Definitely" has a stronger meaning.'

Jimmy raised his hand. 'The grass is definitely green.'

'Very good, Jimmy, but sometimes the grass is brown, or yellow.'

Little Abie waved his hand. 'Yes?' said the teacher.

'Teacher, does a fart have lumps?'

The teacher was horrified. 'Abie, what are you talking about? Of course not!'

'Well then,' said Abie, 'I definitely have shit in my pants.'

Why are the starship *Enterprise* and toilet paper similar?

They both circle Uranus looking for Klingons.

•

How can you tell a macho woman?

She rolls her own tampons.

•

On the first day of kindergarten, the teacher instructed her class on the correct way to get her attention if they had to go to the bathroom.

'Now boys and girls, if you have to make a sissy you raise one finger, and if you have to move your bowels you raise two. Does everybody understand?'

Everybody nods their heads in unison.

All seems to be well. Then about a week later the teacher looks up to see a child frantically waving his hand.

'Why Johnny! What on earth is the matter!'

'Give me a number quick! I gotta fart!'

•

Farmer Johnson was drunk again.

'You know, Anna,' he said to his long-suffering wife, 'if you could only lay eggs we could get rid of all those smelly chickens.'

Anna said nothing. Farmer Johnson tried again.

'You know, Anna, if only you could give milk we could get rid of that expensive herd of cows.'

Anna looked at him coolly. 'You know, Jack,' she said, 'if only you could get it up we could get rid of your brother Bob.'

•

What do you call a child raised in a house of ill repute?

A brothel sprout.

What do the Rockettes and the circus have in common?

The circus is a cunning array of stunts.

•

How would you describe a cow after an abortion?

De-calf-inated.

•

A drunk walks into a bar and says to the bartender, 'If I can make my ass sing, do I get a free drink?' The bartender says sure. The drunk jumps up on the bar and takes a disgusting dump. The patrons go screaming out into the streets. The bartender is furious. 'Why the hell did you do that?!!' he screams. The drunk responds, 'Hey, even Perry Como has to clear his throat.'

•

How can you tell if a woman is wearing panty-hose?

Her ankles swell when she farts.

•

A contest was being held at the circus: a hundred-dollar prize was being offered to the first person who could make the elephant nod his head up and down.

Dozens of people tried and failed. Finally, a little old man walked over to the elephant and grabbed its balls; the elephant roared in pain and tossed its head up and down. The old man collected his prize money and departed.

The next year a similar contest was held using the same elephant; the difference was that the winner had to make the animal shake its head from side to side. Again dozens tried and failed. Finally, the same little old man who walked off with the money the previous year appeared. He walked up to the elephant.

'Remember me?' he said.

The elephant shook its head up and down.

'Want me to do what I did to you last year?'
The elephant shook its head back and forth violently.
The man walked off with the prize money.

●

What do you get when a canary flies into a screen door?

Shredded tweet.

●

Tom met his friend Brent on the street.
    'How are you doing?' asked Tom.
    'Not good,' answered Brent. 'I've had a sore throat for weeks.'
    'Really?' asked Tom. 'I had that same problem a while back.'
    'No kidding,' said Brent. 'How'd you get rid of it?'
    'Well,' replied Tom, 'don't laugh, but my wife gave me a blow job, and it went away like that.'
    'That's great!' responded Brent. 'Do you think she's home now?'

●

How do you get a tissue to dance?

Blow a little boogie into it.

●

What happens when you cross an elephant and a prostitute?

You get a hooker who does it for peanuts and doesn't forget you.

●

Michael was a handsome young man with a terrible problem: severe flatulence. On his first date with a stunning young woman, he was able to control himself for most of the evening, but finally, he needed desperately to get home. Unfortunately, his date insisted that he come home with her to meet her parents.

Sitting in the living room with the family dog, Baron, at his side, Michael could no longer fight nature. He let out an audible fart.

'Baron!' yelled the father.

Thank God, thought Michael.

Not too many minutes passed before Michael had to relieve himself again.

'Baron!' yelled the father again.

Michael relaxed. But nature would not be denied, and this time he really let one roar.

'Baron!' screamed the father. 'Get away from that man before he shits all over you!'

●

Why did they kick the midget out of the nudist colony?

He was getting into everybody's hair.

●

What do a coffin and a condom have in common?

They're both filled with stiffs - only one's coming and one's going.

●

What's brown and sits on a piano bench?

Beethoven's first movement.

●

What's brown and has holes in it?

Swiss shit.

●

Why did the man with the legless dog call his pet 'Cigarette?'

Because every so often he'd take him for a drag.

●

A very attractive, well-dressed man was having a great night picking up women at a midtown bar. A drunk at the other end of the bar, viewing the man's success, was impressed. After the man returned from his third conquest of the evening, the drunk sat next to him and asked him for his secret for picking up women.

'It's easy,' said the man. 'I just smile and say "Tickle your ass with a feather?" If she likes the idea, I'm in. If she says "Excuse me?", I say "It's starting to trickle outside; awfully nasty weather," then move on to someone else.'

'Got ya,' says the drunk.

Half an hour later, the man had left and the drunk had finished another half quart of Scotch. Having spotted his quarry, the drunk staggered up to the woman and said loudly, 'Stick a feather up your ass?'

Shocked, she replied, 'Excuse me?'

'I said,' said the drunk, 'it's raining like a fuck outside.'

●

How do you know that a female bartender is pissed off at you?

There's a string hanging out of your Bloody Mary.

●

Mr. Hudson came home to find his wife sitting naked in front of the mirror, admiring her breasts.

'What do you think you're doing?' he asked.

'I went to the doctor today and he said I have the breasts of a twenty-five-year-old.'

'Oh, yeah? And what did he have to say about your fifty-year-old ass?'

'Nothing,' she replied. 'Your name didn't come up at all.'

●

When it was time for milk and biscuits at the nursery school, Joey refused to line up with the rest of the class.

'What's the matter, Joey?' asked the teacher. 'Don't you want any biscuits today?'

'Fuck you and your milk and biscuits,' Joey answered.

Shocked, the teacher figured the best way to handle the incident was to ignore it. But the next day when it came time for milk and biscuits she got the same reply: 'Fuck you and your milk and biscuits.'

This time the teacher called Joey's mother. She came to class the next day, and when milk and biscuits time arrived she hid in the closet.

The teacher asked Joey if he wanted his snack and he replied: 'Fuck you and your milk and biscuits.'

She opened the closet door and asked Joey's mother what she thought of her son's vulgar language.

'Well, fuck him, don't give him any!'

●

What's the difference between a pigmy tribe and an all-girl track team?

Pigmies are cunning runts.

●

What's green and slides down the hospital walls?

Mucus Welby.

●

Four nuns were outside the confessional, waiting their turn to ask forgiveness for their sins. The first nun went in and said, 'Forgive me Father, for I have sinned. I have put my finger on a man's penis.'

The priest said, 'Say five Our Fathers and put your finger in holy water.'

The second nun went in and said, 'Forgive me Father, for I have sinned. I have put my hand on a man's penis.'

The priest said, 'Say five Our Fathers and put your hand in holy water.'

When she heard this, the third nun turned to the fourth and said, 'Maybe you should go in first, Sister, since I'll have to douche after you gargle.'

●

What's grosser than gross?

When you kiss your grandmother and she slips you the tongue.

●

During the science lesson the teacher asked her third-graders if they could tell her how a cat's tail was connected to its body.

'How about you, Jimmy?' said the teacher. 'Come up here and use the model on my desk.'

Little Jimmy approached the model and studied it thoroughly.

'Well, by the look of those nuts I'd say the damn thing's bolted on!'

●

A man gets drunk at a party, and his friends call a cab to take him home. Once in the cab, the man starts to tell the cabby about his life: how lonely he's been since his wife left him, how hard his job is, how no one appreciates him. 'You seem like a nice guy,' the drunk says.

'Yeah,' says the cabby indifferently.

'What do you say? Do you think there's room in the front seat for a pizza and a couple of six-packs?'

The driver thinks about it for a minute and says, 'Sure, why not?'

'Gee, thanks,' says the drunk, leans over the partition and throws up.

●

How do you find a foxhole?

Lift its tail.

•

What's green and flies over Berlin?

Snotzies.

•

What is this?

O
B.A.
M.A.
PhD.

Three degrees below zero.

•

What is this a picture of?

Two men walking abreast.

•

What's so great about being a test-tube baby?

You have a womb with a view.

•

A man walks into a bar and asks the bartender for a shot of forty-year-old Scotch. Not wanting to go down to the basement and deplete his supply of the rare and expensive liquor, the bartender pours a shot of ten-year-old Scotch and figures that his customer won't be able to tell the difference.

The man downs the Scotch and says, 'My good man, that Scotch is only ten years old. I specifically asked for forty-year-old Scotch.'

Amazed, the bartender reaches into a locked cabinet underneath the bar and pulls out a bottle of twenty-year-old Scotch and pours the man a shot. The customer drinks it down and says, 'That was twenty-year-old Scotch. I asked for forty-year-old Scotch.'

So the bartender goes into the back room and brings out a bottle of thirty-year-old Scotch and pours the customer a drink. By now a small crowd has gathered around the man and is watching anxiously as he downs the latest drink. Once again the man states the true age of the Scotch and repeats his original request.

The bartender can hold off no longer and disappears into the cellar to get a bottle of prime forty-year-old Scotch. As the bartender returns with the drink, an old drunk who had been watching the proceedings with interest leaves the bar and returns with a full shot glass of his own.

The customer downs the Scotch and says, 'Now this is forty-year-old Scotch!' The crowd applauds his discriminating palate.

'I bet you think you're real smart,' slurs the drunk. 'Here, take a swig of this.'

Rising to the challenge, the man takes the glass and downs the drink in one swallow. Immediately, he chokes and spits out the liquid on the barroom floor.

'My God!' he exclaims. 'That's piss!'

'Great guess,' says the drunk. 'Now tell me how old I am.'

●

What do you call a limbless man in a pool?

Bob.

●

What do you call a limbless man on a wall?

Art.

●

What do you call a limbless man in a pile of leaves?

Russell.

●

What do you call a limbless man on a doorstep?

Matt.

●

What's a real friend?

Someone who will go downtown, get two blow jobs, come back and give you one.

●

With his thirtieth wedding anniversary only a week away, Mr. Fairweather stopped in at the best furrier in town.

'I'd like to speak to Al,' said Mr. Fairweather, who knew that Al owned the posh store.

'I'm Al,' said the man standing near a rack of dark furs. 'What can I do for you?'

'Well,' said Mr. Fairweather, 'next week's my thirtieth anniversary, and I want to buy my wife the best fur in town.'

Mr. Fairweather did not look all that wealthy, so Al said, 'How about a lovely raccoon coat?'

'No,' replied Mr. Fairweather. 'My wife got one of those on our tenth anniversary.'

'Well, how about a nice ranch mink?'

'Sorry,' said Mr. Fairweather. 'She got that on our twentieth. Do you have something more interesting - more out of the ordinary?'

'Well,' suggested Al, 'we do have something a bit unusual. How would your wife like a full-length skunk coat?'

'Skunk! Isn't that a rodent?'

'Nah,' replied Al. 'It's just a pussy that smells bad.'

'Thanks anyway,' said Mr. Fairweather. 'She's got one of those too!'

●

Why do women have two holes so close together?

In case you miss.

●

A man goes into a restaurant and orders soup. When the waiter brings out the bowl he has his thumb stuck in the soup, but the customer decides to let this pass.

'Would you like anything else?' the waiter inquires. 'We have some very good beef stew today.'

'Sounds good,' says the customer. So the waiter goes off and comes back with a plate of stew, and his thumb is in the stew. The customer is getting angry, but decides to hold his tongue.

'How about some hot apple pie?' asks the waiter.

'Fine,' says the customer. The waiter returns, with his thumb stuck in the pie. Now the customer is really getting furious.

'Coffee?' asks the waiter, and when the customer nods yes, he hurries off. He returns with his thumb stuck in the cup of coffee. By now the customer can no longer restrain himself.

'What the hell do you think you're doing? Every time you've come to the table you've had your thumb stuck in my food!'

'I've got an infection and my doctor told me to keep my thumb in a hot moist place.'

'Why don't you just stick it up your ass?'

'Where do you think I put it when I'm in the kitchen?'

●

What species of deer is found near pickle factories?

Dill does.

●

John walks into the bar to look for his friend Bob. After finding him, he proceeds to tell him how much he hates his wife.

'Why don't you have her murdered?' asks Bob. 'I know a guy, Artie, who'll do it for you cheap.'

This sounds good to John, so Bob sets up a meeting. Artie and John come to an understanding; they agree on a date, a time, and the fee of a dollar.

Artie goes to John's apartment as planned and strangles John's wife. Unfortunately, the maid walks in before he can escape; Artie strangles her so there will be no witnesses. On his way down the stairs he encounters John's mother-in-law; she, too, has got to go.

Unfortunately for Artie, someone tipped off the police, and he is captured as he walks out the front door.

The next day's headlines read: ARTIE CHOKES THREE FOR A DOLLAR.

●

How do you recycle a used tampon?

As a tea-bag for vampires.

●

What's the difference between a woman kneeling in prayer and a woman kneeling in the bathtub?

The woman kneeling in prayer has hope in her soul.

●

When an elderly couple came into the judge's chamber and asked for a divorce, the judge was totally appalled. 'I cannot believe that you're here in my court. You people are 94 years old and you've been married for 63 years. Why didn't you divorce years ago if you were unhappy? I simply don't understand it.'

The wife looks at the husband, and the husband looks at the wife. Finally the husband turns to the judge and says,

'Well, Judge, we decided to wait until the kids were all dead.'

●

What do you call an adolescent rabbit?

A pubic hare.

●

A priest wanted to raise money for the Church: he was told that there was a fortune in horse racing so he decided to purchase a horse and enter it in a race. However, at an auction, the going price for a horse was so steep that he decided to buy a donkey and race him. To his surprise, the donkey came in third. The next day the racing sheet carried the headlines 'PRIEST'S ASS SHOWS'.

The priest was pleased with the donkey and entered it in a race again. This time it won. The papers read 'PRIEST'S ASS OUT IN FRONT'.

The bishop was so upset with this kind of publicity that he ordered the priest not to enter the donkey in any more races. The newspaper read 'BISHOP SCRATCHES PRIEST'S ASS'.

This was just too much for the bishop so he ordered the priest to get rid of the donkey. The priest gave the donkey to a nun at a nearby convent and the headlines read, 'NUN HAS BEST ASS IN TOWN'.

The bishop fainted. He informed the nun that she would have to dispose of the donkey. She sold it to a farmer for ten dollars. The papers read, 'NUN PEDDLES ASS FOR TEN BUCKS'.

They buried the bishop the next day.

●

What's the last thing that goes through a cat's mind as it's hit by a truck at 100 m.p.h.?

His asshole.

●

What do you call a man with a green ball in each hand?

Someone in perfect control of the Jolly Green Giant.

•

A little boy walked into an ice-cream shop wearing a cowboy hat and a pair of six-shooters. He asked the assistant for an ice-cream sundae.

The assistant asked, 'Do you want your nuts crushed?'

The little boy whipped out his guns, pointed them at her, and said, 'Do you want your tits shot off?'

•

What do you get when you cross a whore with a computer?

A fucking know-it-all.

•

A visibly shaken man staggers into a bar. He asks the barman for a double Scotch. After downing the first drink, he proceeds to down two more doubles. The bartender becomes concerned and asks the man what his problem is. The man mumbles that it's not important, that no one can help him anyway. The man then orders his fourth drink, and again the barman asks if there is anything he can do.

This time the man says, 'Yes, there is something you can do. Answer me a question, how big is a penguin?'

The barman holds his hand about three feet off the ground and says, 'About this high. Why?'

'Shit, I think I've just run over a nun, that's why.'

•

A travelling salesman's car breaks down so he goes for help to a nearby farmhouse. He sees a little boy in the front yard and asks where his mother is. The boy nods his head in a beckoning motion and leads the salesman towards the back yard. The salesman gets there only to find the mother making out with a goat.

Revolted, he turns to the boy and says, 'Do you know what your mother is doing?'

The little boy just nods his head yes.

'Well, doesn't it bother you?'

'NAA NAA NAA NAA. . .'

●

What's black, pink, and hairy and sits on a wall?

Humpty Cunt.

●

The town drunk was always cadging drinks at the local bar. The barman, getting tired of his begging, told him that he would give him a free drink if he would take a sip out of the spitoon.

The drunk, wanting a drink badly, picked up the spitoon and gulped and gulped and gulped. Setting up his drink, the barman remarked that he only wanted him to take a sip.

Downing his drink, the drunk replied, 'I know, but it was in one long string.'

●

Where do female co-pilots sit in an aircraft?

In the cuntpit.

●

What do you call a female peacock?

A peacunt.

●

A young man who could never hold on to his money went off to college one day. But only a month later his money is gone, and he must ask his father for more. His father agrees to send more but warns him to be careful since no more will be sent. Sure enough, though, the boy spends everything and tries to think of a scheme to get more from his father.

Remembering that his father would do just about anything for the family dog, the boy calls his father and says, 'Dad, for £500 there's a professor here who will teach Baron to speak.' After some persuasion the father agrees to send Baron for speech lessons.

A couple of months go by and again the young man runs out of money so he calls his father again. But this time he says, 'Dad, Baron did really well with the speech lessons so the professor feels Baron is ready for the next step. For another £500 he'll teach Baron to read.' Again his father is persuaded, and the money arrives.

The year finally ends and the boy makes plans to come home, but of course Baron cannot speak nor read. Desperate, the boy gives Baron away to a nice family and then makes a phone-call to his dad.

'Dad, I've got some bad news for you, but it's a little bit of a story, so sit down. I was in the bathroom shaving, and Baron was next to me reading *The Times*, when suddenly he says "Hey, do you think your mother will ever find out about all the times Dad fucked around with his secretary?"'

'Dad, I got so nervous that my hand slipped, and the razor flew out of my hand. I don't know how it happened but the razor slit Baron's throat and he's dead.'

After a brief silence his father asked, 'Are you sure?'

●

Mrs. McDonald was known for her Boston Bean soup. When her secret for success was asked for, she replied that she used only 239 beans.

'How come only 239?'

'Because one more would make it too farty.'

●

The emperor was trying to find the best samurai swordsman in the land, so he had a contest. Only three samurai were confident enough to compete. The emperor looked over the three strong men and said 'I have here, in each of three containers, a fly. When I let the fly out of the container, each samurai is to kill the fly as quickly as possible.' All three nodded their understanding and assent.

The first samurai stood up, and the emperor opened the lid of the container. Out buzzed a fly and *whoosh*, quicker than you could imagine, the fly fell to the ground, deftly split in two. The crowd that had gathered in the court applauded.

The second samurai stood, and the emperor opened the lid of the second container. Out buzzed another fly. Even quicker than the first samurai, the second whirled his sword *whoosh whoosh*, and the fly fell to the earth in four pieces. The crowd cheered.

As the third samurai rose to the challenge, everyone wondered what he could do to top the feats of the last two swordsmen. When the emperor opened the lid of the third container, the samurai, poised for action, made a graceful wave of the sword, and the fly buzzed off.

The emperor, furious to think he was being mocked, cried, 'What do you think you're doing? That fly got away!'

'I know,' replied the samurai, 'but he never fuck again!'

●

What do you get when you cross a whore and a Smurf?

A fucking little kid three feet high.

●

A woman comes running into her town sheriff's office screaming in fright.

'Sheriff, the ape from the circus escaped, and it's on my roof!'

'I know just the guy to call.' The sheriff says. 'We'll be right over.'

In less than ten minutes the sheriff and another fellow arrive. The man is carrying a pair of handcuffs and a shotgun, and is leading a very mean looking dog. As they arrive, they spot their quarry. The sheriff turns to the man and says, 'Okay, what's the plan?'

'Well,' says the guy, 'I'll go up on the roof, make some kind of disturbance, and try to scare him off the roof. When the ape falls off the roof, the dog is trained to run right up to him and bite his nuts off. The ape will be in such terrible pain that you can just walk up to him and handcuff him. That's all there is to it.'

The sheriff then says, 'Well, that sounds pretty easy, but what's the shotgun for?'

'That's in case I fall off the roof first – you're going to shoot that fucking dog!'

●

Why do babies have soft spots on their heads?

So in case there's a fire at the hospital, the nurses can carry them out five to a hand.

●

What's brown and sounds like a bell?

Dung.

●

What do you call a female sex-change operation?

Addadicktoomy.

●

A couple are driving along a road one night, when the boy says they have run out of petrol. As they pull off the road, he says to the girl that he might as well take a leak while they've stopped. As he gets out the girl thinks to herself that this all may be some kind of scheme to get her alone in the back seat. She decides to check out whether there is petrol while he is pissing behind the car, so she goes around to the fuel tank nozzle. Opening it, she tries to smell for fumes. Smelling none, she strikes a match.

BAM! The tank blows and the couple are blown into the bushes.

Coming to, the girl says, 'Help me find my purse, it has my money in it.'

The boy moans, 'Aw, fuck your purse, help me find my hand. It has my prick in it!'

●

# Racial Mixtures

What's the difference between an Irishman and a black man?

The black man takes the dishes out of the sink before he pisses in it.

•

Why can't you circumcise an Arab?

Because there's no end to those pricks.

•

Did you hear about the new German microwave oven?

It seats six.

•

A Texas businessman arrives at his hotel in the heart of a major Japanese city. He arranges to have a beautiful Japanese prostitute be his companion for the night.

The woman arrives, and is more beautiful and sensual than he had imagined; once in bed he takes her with great enthusiasm and unbridled lust. During the act he hears his partner cry out many times, 'Sung wha! Sung wha!'

'That must be Japanese for "terrific",' thinks the Texan, 'because I can tell from the way she's thrashing around she's never been had like this before.'

The next morning, the Texan has an appointment with two very important Japanese business associates to play golf. Naturally he wants to impress the men with his friendliness and goodwill, so when the older gentleman makes a hole in one, the Texan shouts, 'Sung wha! Sung wha!'

The Japanese turns, eyebrows raised in surprise. 'Wrong hole? What you mean, wrong hole?'

●

Did you hear about the queer Irishman?

He liked women better than whisky.

●

The Frenchman at the beach was surrounded by beautiful women. He was watched enviously by an Irishman sitting all alone.

When the Frenchman got up to get a drink, the Irishman followed him.

'Excuse me, sir,' the Irishman said, 'but I couldn't help noticing how women are attracted to you. Would you mind revealing your secret?'

Smiling, the Frenchman said, 'It's simple. I put a potato in my bathing suit. It drives the women wild.'

'Thanks, I'll try it,' said the Irishman, and he hurried away.

Three days later the Irishman again met the Frenchman at the beach.

'Hey! I thought you said that if I put a potato in my bathing suit it would drive the women wild. I've had one there for three days and women are going out of their way to avoid me!'

The Frenchman eyed the Irishman and said, 'Try putting it in the front.'

●

Why do they call camels the ships of the desert?

Because they're full of Arab semen.

●

Three foreign legionnaires – a Jew, an Italian, and a Pole – were to be flogged for disobeying orders. Their sergeant, not wishing to be unnecessarily cruel, asked each man if they wanted anything put on their backs to help them bear their punishment.

The Italian requested olive oil. It was applied to his skin, and he was whipped within an inch of his life.

The Pole said, 'I am strong like bull. I need nothing.' He too was whipped unmercifully, but didn't utter a sound.

The Jew, who had witnessed both whippings, was then asked what he wanted on his back. After a minute of thought he replied, 'The Pole.'

●

What do you call an abortion in Czechoslovakia?

A cancelled czech.

●

Did you hear about the new Mexican war movie?

It's called Tacolipsnow.

●

An American vacationing in Spain goes into a restaurant near the bullring. He doesn't know enough of the language to read the menu, but notices that the man at the next table is being served an extraordinary dish. The waiter has lifted a large silver dome to reveal two big beefy filets smothered in sautéed onions and an exquisite sauce.

The American calls the waiter over and asks what the dish is.

'It is the house speciality, *señor*,' the waiter replies.

'Fine, I'll have that.'

'I am very sorry, *señor*, but there is only one portion prepared each day. If you like, we can reserve tomorrow's portion for you. The bullfight is over at three; you may come for dinner any time after four.'

The American reserves his dinner and leaves.

The next day he returns after four, as specified, and requests the house speciality. The waiter brings out a silver-domed platter and lifts the cover, revealing a dish full of sautéed onions, the same exquisite sauce, and two small round nuggets of meat. Furious, the American says to the waiter, 'This isn't the same dish you served yesterday! What happened to those huge filets?'

'Many pardons, *señor*,' the waiter says, 'but sometimes the bull wins.'

●

What's the difference between an Irish wedding and an Irish funeral?

One less drunk.

●

What's Greek foreplay?

Here, sheepie, sheepie, sheepie.

●

Why don't Mexicans barbecue?

Because the beans slip through the grill.

●

What's the German word for 'bra?'

Stopemfromfloppen.

●

Why did the Greek boy leave his homeland?

He didn't like the way he was being reared.

And why did he return?

He couldn't leave his brother's behind.

●

During the French Revolution, three men were sentenced to the guillotine. One was a Frenchman, one was an Englishman, and the third was an Irishman.

The Frenchman takes his place on the block and the blade is released. On the way down, it jams. Traditionally, if the guillotine fails, the condemned man is pardoned. So the Frenchman is set free.

Seeing this happen strikes a spark of hope in the two remaining prisoners. The Englishman takes his place at the guillotine. Again the machine malfunctions and the Englishman is set free.

Now it's the Irishman's turn. But as he is being led to the platform he begins to struggle and scream. 'I'm not going near that thing until you get it fixed!'

●

A reporter walked up to Stevie Wonder and asked him how it felt to have been born blind.

Stevie replied, 'It could've been worse, I could have been born black!'

●

What do you have when two blacks are in a shoe-box?

A pair of black loafers.

●

A black man in the deep South died and started walking to heaven. In front of him, the road split. One sign read 'Straight to Heaven'; the other said 'To Purgatory'. He strolled right up to the Pearly Gates.

'Just a minute!' said St. Peter. 'You have to have done something pretty special to go straight to heaven. What have you done?'

'I married a white woman on the courthouse steps in Mobile, Alabama,' the black man proudly replied.

'That is pretty special,' agreed St. Peter. 'When did you do that?'

'Oh, about three minutes ago.'

Did you hear about the little black boy who had diarrhoea?

He jumped into his mother's freezer 'cause he thought he was melting.

●

What's black and red and has trouble getting through a revolving door?

An African with a spear through his back.

●

Did you hear about Ku Klux Knievel?

He tried to jump over eight black men with a steamroller.

●

The body of a black civil liberties worker, which was wrapped in chains, was pulled out of a lake in the deep South. The local newspaper reporter asked the sheriff for his thoughts on the case. The sheriff replied, 'Shoot! Ain't that just like a black boy, stealing more chains than he could swim with.'

●

How do you get a black man out of a tree in Alabama?

Cut the rope.

●

Why do blacks always have sex on their minds?

Because they have pubic hair on their heads.

●

An American black woman was washing her clothes in a pasture stream. She was leaning over a scrubbing board, her skirt tied up so it wouldn't get wet; her devil red panties were showing.

A bull in the pasture caught sight of the panties and charged. WHAM! The woman kept on with her wash, and said calmly, 'I don't know who you is and I don't know where you come from, but I'm here every Monday, Wednesday, and Friday!'

●

What do you call a black prostitute with braces?

A Black & Decker pecker wrecker.

●

Did you hear about the new war movie in production with an all-black cast?

A Pack of Lips, Now.

●

Two black G.I.s are promoted to sergeant. They decide to celebrate by going into town and getting laid. After they find a prostitute they both like, they follow her back to her room. As they're getting undressed, she says, 'Look, I want to be honest with you; I have gonorrhea.'

Neither man knows what gonorrhea is, so one goes to get a dictionary and look it up. He returns a few minutes later and says, 'No problem. Let's get on with it!'

A few weeks later, both men start to burn and discharge. They go to the camp doctor who informs them that they both have the clap.

'I thought you looked that word up,' says the first man.

'I did, and I could have sworn we were safe!'

'Why? What did it say?'

'It said, "Gonorrhea: a disease of the privates."'

●

Why do blacks make such good hurdlers?

They're raised jumping turnstiles.

What's this?

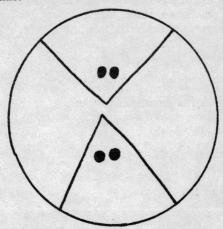

The last thing a Southern black man sees after being thrown into a well.

Why do Jewish women use tampons instead of sanitary napkins?

Because nothing goes in without a string attached.

A rich American Jewish girl goes to her doctor to get some relief from the bruises she has on her knees.

'Those bruises are awful. How did you get them?' asks the doctor.

Embarrassed, the girl answers, 'Well, you see, doctor, when we, er, make love, er, well. . .'

'Oh, I understand,' said the doctor. 'You'll just have to change positions until those bruises heal.'

'Oh no, doctor, I can't do that. My dog's breath is murder!'

One day a man goes to his Jewish wife and wants to know how much she loves him.

'Darling,' he asks, 'would you still love me if I became disfigured?'

'I'll always love you,' she says as she files her nails.

'How about if I couldn't make love to you any more?'

'I'll always love you, dear,' she replies as she concentrates on her nails.

'Well, how about if I lost my £40,000 a year job? Would you still love me then?'

The wife puts down her nail file, looks at her husband's anxious face and says, 'Darling, I'll always love you, but most of all I'll really miss you!'

•

Sadie Feingold was on safari. She was taking pictures when a huge gorilla swung down out of a tree and carried her off to his lair where he used and abused her in ways she had never even heard about. Luckily, a rescue party found her while her captor was in search of a banana, and took her back to civilization. While she was recuperating in the hospital, her best friend came to visit. 'Sadie! Such a terrible experience, but at least you're alive.' Sadie was silent. 'Sadie! Say something!'

'Say? What's there to say? It's been two weeks; he doesn't call, he doesn't write . . .'

•

Mr. Greenstein went to the doctor.

'So what's your problem?' the doctor asked.

'I can't pee,' Greenstein replied.

'Hmmm. How old are you?'

'Eighty-one.'

'Don't you think you've peed enough?'

•

How can you tell when a Jewish woman has an orgasm?

She drops her nail file.

•

The first Martian expedition landed on Earth and was met by the press. A reporter looked at one of the Martians and said, 'I see you have a pointed head. Does everyone on Mars have a pointed head?'

The Martian looked at him as though he were crazy, and said, 'Of course.'

'I see you have bright green hands and feet. On Earth, this is very unusual. Does everyone on Mars have green hands and feet?'

The Martian replied, 'Of course.'

'You're wearing an enormous amount of gold jewellery,' the reporter said. 'Rings, bracelet, necklaces – I've never seen so much gold on one person before. Does everyone on Mars wear that much jewellery?'

'Not the *goyim*.'

•

Old Mr. Goldberg, after eating a seven-course meal in a restaurant, announced to the waiter that he wasn't going to pay the bill because he'd found a hair in his rice pudding.

The waiter insisted that Mr. Goldberg pay the bill, but Mr. Goldberg ran out of the restaurant. The waiter, angered, ran after him. He didn't catch up with him until Mr. Goldberg had reached the neighbourhood brothel.

The waiter explained to the madam that he must talk to Mr. Goldberg – could she please point out the room into which he had disappeared? The waiter slipped her a couple of quid, and the madam pointed down the hall.

The waiter rushed into the indicated room to find Mr. Goldberg eating one of the girls. The waiter said, 'For a hair in your rice pudding you won't pay your bill, but you'll come to this place and eat her?!'

'That's right,' answered the old Jew. 'And if I find rice pudding in her, I'm not paying her, either.'

●

Mrs. Goldblum brought her husband's remains to the undertaker to have cremated. When asked what kind of container she wanted his ashes stored in, she said, 'None. I want them poured right into my hands.'

The undertaker thought this rather odd, but did as the widow requested. Mrs. Goldblum returned home and went straight to the bedroom. She dimmed the lights, put romantic music on the stereo, and whispered, 'Hymie, here's that blow job you always wanted!' And she blew his ashes all over the bed.

●

How does a Jewish couple perform 'doggie-style' sex?

He sits up and begs and she lies down and plays dead.

●

# In A Word, Sex

Did you hear about the little boy who, while passing his parents' bedroom, stared in and said, 'And you have the nerve to slap me for sucking my thumb!'

●

An old whore walks into a bar with a parrot on her finger.
   'I'll fuck the first guy here who can guess this parrot's weight!'
   After a long silence a drunk in the back yells out, 'Five hundred pounds!'
   'Close enough!'

●

What do Rubik's Cube and a penis have in common?

The longer you play with it, the harder it gets.

●

What's a 68?

You do me and I owe you one.

●

Sally arrived home from her date on a cloud. She tossed her coat over a chair, her handbag over the banister; she threw the rest of her clothing around her bedroom with abandon.
   The next morning at breakfast her mother asked if she had a good time.

'Oh,' sighed Sally, 'I had a *wonderful* time!'

'I guess so,' her mother remarked. 'Your knickers are still stuck to the ceiling.'

●

What's the modern woman's idea of the perfect man?

One who's two-and-a-half feet tall, has a ten-inch tongue, and can breathe through his ears.

●

A boy baby and a girl baby are lying together in their crib. All of a sudden, the girl baby starts to scream, 'Rape! Rape! Somebody help me! Rape! Rape!'

Her companion looks at her and says, 'Oh, shut up! You just rolled over on my dummy.'

●

What's the difference between men and jelly beans?

Jelly beans come in different colours.

●

A man spending the afternoon with his married lover hears her husband return unexpectedly. He hops out of bed, grabs his clothes, and ducks into the wardrobe. Behind him he hears a whisper, 'Boy, it's dark in here!'

'Who's that?'

'My name's Johnny, and I live here. Do you want to buy my marble collection? Only fifty pounds.'

'Fifty pounds? Are you crazy?' asks the man.

'Well, if you're not interested maybe my father –'

'No, wait! Here's the fifty, now shut up!'

Two days later, in the same bed, the man hears his lover's husband return. Again he takes cover in the wardrobe, and hears a small voice behind him say, 'Boy, it's dark in here!'

'You again?'

'Yes, and this time I'm selling my football card collection.'

'Okay, how much this time?'

'One hundred. Inflation, you know.'

'Jesus! Here. Now shut up!'

The next day the boy boasts about his windfall to his father, who says, 'I don't know what you did to get that much money, but it couldn't have been honest. You'd better go to confession.'

So the boy goes to church and takes his place in the confessional. He says in a whisper, 'Boy, it's dark in here!'

At that the priest's partition opens with a bang, and the priest says, 'Are you going to start that shit again?'

●

Why isn't being a penis all it's cracked up to be?

You have a head but no brains, there are always a couple of nuts following you around all the time, your nextdoor neighbour is an asshole, and your best friend is a cunt.

●

A horny pair of teenagers are driving down the highway; they can't keep their hands off one another. The young man, very aroused, says to his girlfriend, 'Let's pull over and do it by the side of the road.'

'But people driving by will be able to see into the car,' she protests.

The boy pulls over on an incline off the highway. 'Look, we'll get underneath the car, and I'll leave my feet sticking out. If anyone comes by I'll tell them I'm fixing the silencer.'

Reluctantly, the girl agrees, so they wriggle underneath the car and start to make love. All of a sudden, the young man feels someone kicking his foot.

And just what do you think you're doing?' a policeman asks.

'Fixing my silencer,' the boy replies.

'Well, you should have fixed your brakes first; your car's just rolled down the hill.'

●

How many mice does it take to screw in a light bulb?

Two, but don't ask me how they got there.

•

What's the difference between kinky and perverted?

Kinky is when you tickle your lover's ass with a feather. Perverted is when you use the whole chicken.

•

Mrs. Schwartz decided she should learn to play golf. She signed up for lessons with the pro at the country club, but after six months she could still barely get the ball off the tee. At the end of his patience, the pro finally said, 'Mrs. Schwartz, there's only one thing left that I can think of to try with you. No matter how strange my instructions sound, just do what I say. I want you to hold the club as though it were your husband's penis, and hit the ball.' This was indeed strange, but Mrs. Schwartz was willing to try anything. She followed the pro's instructions and, lo and behold, the ball went 300 yards straight down the fairway. 'Wonderful!' said the pro. 'Now take the club out of your mouth –'

•

Why does an elephant have four feet?

Because eight inches isn't enough.

•

What do soyabeans and dildos have in common?

They're both meat substitutes.

•

What has a thousand teeth and holds back a monster?

My fly zip.

•

What do a virgin and a haemophiliac have in common?

One prick and it's all over.

●

How does a woman hold her liquor?

By the ears.

●

Did you hear about the merger of Xerox and Wurlitzer?

The new company will make reproductive organs.

●

The young Indian brave went to his chief and said, 'Me want squaw.'

'Do you have experience?' the chief asked.

'No,' the boy replied. 'How me get experience?'

'Go into the woods, find tree with knothole, and practise. Come back in two weeks and I will give you squaw.'

The boy left and, as instructed, returned in two weeks.

'You have experience?' asked the chief. The boy nodded. 'Good, now you have experience you can have squaw. Little Flower, come here! This brave has no experience with woman. You treat him well and guide him.'

Smiling, Little Flower took the young brave by the hand and led him to her teepee. There, after they had undressed, the brave told Little Flower to turn around and bend over. Puzzled, she complied, then shrieked when he kicked her in the ass.

'What you do that for?' she asked.

'Me no stupid. Me check for bees!'

●

A little boy walked in on his mother while she was taking a bath.

'What's that?' he asked, pointing to her pubic hair.

'It's my face cloth, sweetheart,' she answers.

'Oh yes,' he says, 'I saw the maid washing Daddy's face with one last night.'

●

What's better than four roses on a piano?

Two lips on an organ.

●

What do butter and a hooker have in common?

They both spread for bread.

●

A travelling saleswoman was driving through a remote rural area in the deep South when her car broke down. She started walking and eventually came to a small farmhouse. On the front porch sat two men in rocking chairs.

'How far is it to the nearest petrol station?' she asked.

'Oh, about twenty miles, I reckon,' drawled one man.

'Well, how far is it to the nearest hotel?'

'I guess that would be about thirty miles,' answered his companion.

'Could you drive me there?'

'Don't have no car.'

Despairing the woman said, 'Do you think I could possibly stay with you tonight? I'm sure I'll be able to hitch a ride in the morning.'

'Sure you can. But you'll have to share our bed.'

The woman had no other choice but to agree. Before she got into bed that night, she handed each man a rubber and said, 'Please wear these so I won't get pregnant.'

The next morning she left. Three months later, the two men are sitting on the porch when one says to the other, 'Say, Bob, do you care if that there saleslady gets pregnant?'

'Nope.'

'Then what do you say we take these damn things off.'

●

What's the difference between 'ohh' and 'ahh?'

About four inches.

●

A farmer was having trouble getting his chicken to lay eggs, so he brought in a rooster who had a reputation as (if you will pardon the expression) a legendary cocksman. The rooster got right to work, and soon there were eggs all over the place. His job done, the rooster went after the pigs, the ducks, the sheep, and would have gone after a snake if someone had held its head. The farmer, afraid of losing the bird, tried to get him to calm down, but with no luck. One morning he found the rooster flat on his back, eyes closed - apparently dead of exhaustion. When he started to berate the corpse, the rooster opened one eye and said 'Shh! You see those buzzards up there?'

●

What's organic dental floss?

Pubic hair.

●

When does a Cub become a Boy Scout?

When he eats his first Brownie.

●

Moskowitz, Horowitz, and Shapiro went on safari, where they were set upon by a large tribe of fierce and hostile savages. Bound and helpless, they were brought before the chief. Pointing to Moskowitz, he says, 'You have a choice. Death or bunda.'

Moskowitz says 'What could be worse than death? Bunda!'

He's seized and viciously sodomized by the entire tribe.

The next day the chief says to Horowitz, 'Death or bunda?'

Horowitz, shaking, says, 'Bunda.' He too is abused by the whole tribe.

The next day the chief stands in front of Shapiro and says, 'Death or bunda?' Shapiro looks him straight in the eye and says, 'Death.'

'Terrific!' says the chief. 'Death by bunda!'

●

What do women and spaghetti have in common?

They both squirm when you eat them.

●

What's a 72?

69 with three people watching.

●

What do you call a female clone?

A clunt.

●

Where is an elephant's sex organ?

In his feet: if he steps on you, you're fucked.

●

What did the hurricane say to the coconut tree?

Hold on to your nuts; this ain't gonna be no ordinary blow job.

●

What do you call a happy Roman?

Glad he ate her.

●

On their first date, Joe took Rose to the carnival. When he asked her what she wanted to do first, Rose replied, 'Get weighed.'

So Joe took her to the man with the scale who guesses your weight. He looked at Rose and said, 'One hundred and twenty pounds.' Since Rose weighed in at one seventeen, she collected a prize.

Next they went on to the roller-coaster. When the ride was finished, Joe asked Rose what she wanted to do next. 'Get weighed,' she said. So they went back to the man with the scale, who of course guessed Rose's weight correctly. Leaving without a prize, they went for a ride on the merry-go-round. After they got off, Joe asked Rose what she wanted to do. 'I want to get weighed!' she said again.

Now Joe began to think this girl was quite strange, and decided to end the evening quickly. He left her at the door with a quick handshake.

Rose's roommate was waiting up for her to return and asked how the evening went.

'Wousy!'

●

Is sex better than pot?

It depends on the pusher.

●

Saul, who was three feet, five inches tall, was asked how he had liked his stay at the nudist colony.

'It was a bit scary,' he replied. 'Everyone looked like Fidel Castro.'

●

One sunny day a bunny rabbit was walking along the water's edge when he saw an island. Straining his eyes, the bunny spied what looked like hundreds of thousands of carrot leaves. 'Boy,' thought the bunny, 'if I could just get over to that island, I'd be the happiest bunny in the world.'

Now bunnies hate water, but all those delicious carrots proved a huge temptation to our bunny, and he decided to try to get out to the island. Getting up all his courage, he took three running hops and PLOP! landed right in the middle of the island. What he'd seen from shore were indeed carrot leaves, and he began to munch happily away on all the carrots a rabbit could want. 'I *am* the happiest bunny in the world,' thought the rabbit as he hopped happily along eating carrots.

About half an hour later, a cat was walking along the shore and saw the rabbit hopping happily away on the island. Her eyes not being as good (for she didn't eat carrots), she had no idea that it was all those carrots that were making the bunny so happy. 'Boy,' she thought, 'look how happy that bunny is. If I could just get over to that island, I'd be the happiest cat in the world.'

Cats hate water even more than bunnies do, but our cat was determined to be as happy as that bunny was. Getting up all her courage, she crouched, sprang, and SPLASH! landed in the water and drowned.

The moral of the story: behind every satisfied Peter is a wet pussy.

●

A little boy walks in on his mother while she's taking a bath.

'What's that?' he asks, pointing at his mother's pubic hair.

'That's where Daddy hit me with an axe,' she answers.

Wide-eyed the boy says, 'You mean right in the cunt?!'

●

What do you call a truck full of vibrators?

Toys for twats.

●

Preparing to walk through the dangerous woods to see her grandmother, Little Red Riding Hood puts her father's gun in her picnic basket.

On the way, she is stopped by the Big Bad Wolf.

'Little Red Riding Hood, I'm going to rape you,' growls the wolf.

Drawing her gun Little Red Riding Hood declares, 'Oh, no, you're not. You're going to eat me, just like the story says.'

●

A man walked into a bar with a dog at his side. 'Get that dog out of here,' ordered the barman.

The dog's owner became indignant. 'This isn't just any old dog,' he said. 'He's the smartest dog in the whole world.'

'Oh yeah? Prove it!' challenged the barman.

Turning to the dog, the man said, 'Rex, here's a pound. Go and get me a packet of fags.'

The dog ran out the door and, within a few minutes, returned with the cigarettes and some matches in a little brown bag.

The barman was impressed. 'Maybe that dog *is* really smart. How about if I give him ten pounds and ask him to bring me back a bag of pot from the local dealer?'

'Sure,' said the dog's owner. The barman gave the dog money and directions, and the dog was on his way.

Ten minutes went by.

Half an hour.

After an hour, the dog still hadn't returned.

By this time, the barman, sure he'd been cheated, threw the dog's owner out of the bar.

The man wandered several blocks in search of his errant pet. Finally he came to an alley, and there was Rex screwing a mangy-looking French poodle.

'Why, you son of a bitch,' screamed the man, separating the two dogs. 'You really blew the act this time. How could you do this to me? You've never done anything like this before!'

'True,' replied the dog. 'But I never had ten pounds before, either.'

●

Little Red Riding Hood was walking through the woods when the Big Bad Wolf jumped out of the bushes and said,

'Now I've got you and I'm going to eat you!'

'Eat, eat, eat,' said Little Red Riding Hood. 'Doesn't anybody just fuck anymore?'

●

A really conceited man is screwing a really conceited woman.

'Aren't I tight?' she asks.

'No,' he replies, 'just full.'

●

What's 69 and 69?

Dinner for four.

●

What's the difference between your sister and a Cadillac?

Most people haven't been in a Cadillac.

●

And then there was the man who bought his wife a glass diaphragm because he wanted a womb with a view.

●

What's the difference between a prostitute and a rooster?

A rooster says 'Cock-a-doodle-doo.'

A prostitute says 'Any cock will do.'

●

Two fleas met on the beach in Miami; one of them had a terrible cold.

'What happened to you?' asked his friend.

'I came down on the moustache of a man on a motorcycle.'

'Look, next year, you go to the airport, get on a toilet seat in the stewardesses' lounge, and you'll have a nice soft warm ride down.'

'Sounds good,' wheezed the flea. 'I'll try it.'

The next winter the two fleas met on the beach again; the same flea had a terrible cold again.

'What happened?' asked his friend. 'Didn't you take my advice?'

'Sure I did. I went to the airport, parked myself on a toilet seat in the stewardesses' lounge, and when one sat down, I hopped aboard. It was so soft and warm and comfy that I fell asleep – and woke up on the moustache of a man on a motorcycle.'

●

Why don't chickens need underwear?

Because their peckers are on their faces.

●

What's worse than getting raped by Jack the Ripper?

Being fingered by Captain Hook.

●

What do you call a midget's circumcision?

Tiny trim.

●

Did you hear about the guy who got herpes on his eyelids?

He was looking for love in all the wrong places.

●

A guy was screwing his girlfriend in the back seat of his car when a policeman comes by and says, 'What do you think you're doing?'

The man rolls down his window and answers, 'I'm screwing my girlfriend.'

'Good!' says the policeman. 'I'm next.'

'Sounds good to me,' says the man. 'I've never screwed a cop before.'

A lumberjack went to a brothel and asked for the meanest, toughest girl in the house.

'I know just the girl for you,' said the madam. 'Go ahead upstairs – second room on the left – and I'll send her up.' He started up the stairs.

'Oh,' yelled the madam after him. 'Is there anything else you'd like?'

'Yes,' he replied from the top of the stairs, 'a six-pack of beer would be nice.'

The lumberjack entered the room and sat down. A few minutes later, in came a big bruiser of a woman, naked and carrying a six-pack.

The lumberjack liked what he saw, and couldn't wait to get started. The big woman was just what he was looking for. But before he could make a move for her, she got down on all fours, arched her back, and thrust her ass at him.

Incredibly excited, the lumberjack asked, 'Wow, what's that position called?

'Position? What position?' the big whore replied. 'I thought you'd want to open the beer first.'

●

What do a spider's web and a passionate kiss have in common?

They both end in the undoing of a fly.

●

What do you call a woman who can suck an orange through a garden hose?

Darling.

●

What's worse than a lobster on your piano?

Crabs on your organ.

•

Did you hear about the nympho at the hotel pool?

She was barred from the area after the life-guard saw her go down for the third time.

•

When is it extremely dangerous to have a wet dream?

When you're under an electric blanket.

•

A proud father gave his son twenty pounds and sent him off to the local brothel. On his way the boy passed by his grandmother's house and she called him in. He explained where he was going and she insisted that he save the twenty pounds and make love to her.

The boy returned home with a big smile. 'How was it?' asked the father.

'Great, and I saved the twenty pounds,' responded the boy.

'How's that?' his father asked.

'I did it with Grandma,' the boy explained.

His father screamed, 'You mean you fucked my mother?'

'Hey, why not? You've been fucking mine!'

•

A man works for many years in a pickle factory. He works the machine right next to the pickle slicer. At night he has kinky dreams about the pickle slicer. One day he goes bonkers, and when he thinks no one is looking he starts to kiss the pickle slicer. Lust overpowers his senses and he puts his pecker in the pickle slicer.

At that moment the boss happens to be passing by and sees the man attacking the pickle slicer. The boss calls the man a degenerate and fires him on the spot. The man goes home and his wife asks him what he's doing home so early.

He replies, 'I went crazy and tried to make love to the pickle slicer. The boss saw me and fired me.'

'Oh my God!' screams the wife, and pulls down her husband's pants to inspect the damage. Seeing none, she says, 'Well, thank the lord you weren't hurt, but what happened to the pickle slicer?'

The man smiled sheepishly and said, 'The boss fired her too.'

●

An astronaut lands on Mars and comes across a beautiful Martian woman stirring a huge pot over a flaming fire.

'What are you doing?' he asks her.

'Making babies,' she answers.

'That's not the way we do it on earth,' he tells her.

'Well, how is it done there?' she asks him.

'I can't really explain it, but it's easy to show you. May I?'

She says yes, and he proceeds to show her how it's done. When they're finished she asks, 'So where are the babies?'

'Oh, they don't come for another nine months,' he told her.

'So why did you stop stirring, then?'

●

What's the difference between having a job and being married for ten years?

A job still sucks after ten years.

●

What do you do when your Kotex catches fire?

Throw it on the floor and tampon it.

●

Micky Mouse stood before the judge waiting for the verdict.

'Micky Mouse, I cannot grant you a divorce since the court has found Minnie Mouse to be mentally competent,' proclaimed the judge.

'But, your honour, I didn't say Minnie was crazy. I said she was fucking Goofy!'

●

Two friends are talking at a local bar one night.

'Man, was I lucky last night,' said the first guy.

'What happened. Did you win the lottery or something?' asked the second.

'No,' but last night I was banging my old lady, you know, and right in the middle of everything WHAM! the damn chandelier comes flying down on my ass!'

'You call that lucky?' asks his friend.

'Shit yes, if it had happened a couple of minutes sooner it would have broken my neck!'

●

A plane is flying over the Atlantic Ocean as the pilot is finishing an announcement on the intercom. Putting the mike down he hits the off switch. Unbeknown to him the switch is malfunctioning and his conversation is broadcast into the passenger area.

'Take over for a while, Dave,' the pilot says to his co-pilot, 'I think I'll go take a shit and then bang that new stewardess.'

At this statement the passengers fly into a frenzy of conversation and gossip. The stewardess is greatly embarrassed and can no longer stay at her post, so she hurries towards the cockpit. But in her haste, she trips and falls to her knees in the aisle.

She happens to land next to a sweet little old lady who turns to help her up. As she does so, the lady says sweetly, 'Don't rush, dearie. He said he had to take a shit first.'

●

Ginny and Joe are having a drink in Joe's apartment – their second date – and Joe is pouring Ginny a glass of wine.

'Tell me when,' he says.

'After dinner,' she replies.

●

Do you know how married couples do it doggy style?

Without all the licking and sniffing.

●

A woman who was unhappy with the size of her breasts made an appointment with Dr. Schwartz, a breast specialist. After examining her the doctor gave her a special cream to apply to her breasts.

'Now, listen carefully,' Dr. Schwartz said. 'These directions are very specific and you must apply the cream always the same way. They may sound strange, but believe me, if you do it right, in no time you will be beautiful. Now, take your right hand, put a little cream in your palm, and apply it to your left breast, rubbing in a circular motion. As you are doing this I want you to chant "Mary had a little lamb". Then add more cream to the same hand and move to your right breast, and keep rubbing in that same circular motion. On this breast you must chant "Her fleece was white as snow". Keep rubbing and chanting until all the cream is absorbed. Do this entire procedure exactly as I have shown you, four times a day for a month. When the month is up you will have wonderful breasts.'

So the woman goes home and every four hours she stops whatever she is doing and goes through the procedure. But one day she is in a shopping area and it is time to apply her cream. She runs to the parking area, hops into her car and undoes her blouse. Applying her cream she sings, 'Mary had a little lamb, his fleece was white as snow.'

Suddenly she sees a man in another car staring at her. Smiling, he shouts to her, 'Do you go to Dr. Schwartz?'

Embarrassed, the woman nods her head, yes.

'I thought so. So do I', the man replies.

And as the man turns away busying himself with something in his lap, the woman hears him sing, 'Hickory, dickory, dock, the mouse ran up the clock.'

●

How do you make a hormone?

Don't pay her.

●

You know you're getting old when your wife gives up sex for Lent and you don't find out until after Easter.

●

How do you get a nun pregnant?

Fuck her.

●

Two friends were walking on the beach one day when they saw a peculiar-looking man coming the other way. The stranger had an extraordinarily small head in comparison with the rest of his body.

'Excuse me, sir, I don't mean to be rude but . . .' began the first friend.

'I know what you're going to ask me, and I don't mind telling you about it because it was my own stupid fault,' replied the stranger. 'One summer day, very much like today, I was walking along this very beach. In the sand I saw a very old looking bottle with a cork in it. Being terribly curious, I unplugged it. Sure enough, out comes this beautiful naked genie. She was the sexiest, hottest looking woman I ever saw. So when she said she'd grant me any one wish I desired, I said, 'How about a little head?

●

Confucius say: woman who flies airplane upside-down, has crack up.

•

Why do women rub their eyes when they get out of bed in the morning?

Because they don't have balls to scratch.

•

A precocious nine-year-old walked into a bar and yelled to the waitress to bring him a Scotch on the rocks.

'What do you want to do?' asked the waitress. 'Get me into trouble?'

'Maybe later,' replied the nine-year-old, 'but right now I'd like that drink.'

•

There were three couples who approached the local priest because they wanted to join the Catholic Church. And he said, 'Well, you can join the Church, but to be able to join in good standing you have to abstain from sex for thirty days.' The three couples agreed to this.

When the thirty days were up, the first couple came in and the priest asked, 'How'd you do? And the husband said, 'We did fine, no problems at all.' The priest says, 'Well, that's great. You can come into the Church in good standing.'

The second couple entered and the Father said, 'How'd you do?' The wife said, 'Well, we did pretty well. It was really a tough fight but we did OK.' And the priest said, 'Well, that's just great. You can come into the Church in good standing.'

The third couple came in and when the priest asked how they did, the husband said. 'Well, father, we did fine until the 27th day – then my wife bent over to pick up a head of lettuce. I couldn't stand it any longer, and I just gave it to her right there.' And the priest said, 'Well, I'm sorry, you can't come into the Church in good standing.' And the young man says, 'I know. We can't go back into the supermarket again either.'

•

Why can't gypsies have babies?

Because their husbands have crystal balls.

●

Why can't witches have babies?

Because their husbands have holloweenies.

●

An 85-year-old man went to the doctor for a physical. After examining the man, the doctor said, 'I can hardly believe this! You have the body of a 40-year-old man. You could live quite a long time. How old was your father when he died?'

'Dad's still alive,' replied the patient. 'He's 105 and still works five days a week.'

'Incredible,' said the doctor. 'How old was your grandfather when he died?'

'Grandad's still alive, too. He's 129 years old and going to marry a 22-year-old girl this Saturday.'

'Why ever would a 129-year-old man want to get married?'

'Who said he *wants* to get married?'

●

A little boy accompanied his swinging parents to a nudist colony for the first time. After looking around for a few minutes the boy asked his father why some men had big ones and some men had small ones.

Rather than go into a long explanation the father replied, 'The men that have big ones are smart and the men that have small ones are stupid.'

Accepting his father's explanation, the boy went off to explore his new surroundings. Time passed and he finally came across his father again.

'Where's your mum, son?'

'Oh,' the boy answers, 'she's behind the bushes talking to some stupid guy who's getting smarter by the minute.'

●

How far could you see if you had a twelve-inch prick growing out of your forehead?

You couldn't see at all because the balls would be in your eyes.

●

What is the difference between love and like?

Spit or swallow.

●

# Fruits and Nuts

Define 'organ grinder'.

A gay with a chipped front tooth.

•

Did you hear about the gay bank robber?

He tied up the safe and blew the tellers.

•

How can you separate the men from the boys in a gay bar?

With a crowbar.

•

Two gay lovers were having a quarrel.
  'Go to hell!' screamed one.
  'Drop dead!' screamed the other.
  'Kiss my ass!'
  'Oh, you *do* want to make up!'

•

What do you call a gay with a vasectomy?

A seedless fruit.

•

Did you hear about the two Scottish gays?

Ben Dover and Phil MacCrevice.

A truck driver passing through a small town stopped at a local bar and grill, looking forward to some supper and maybe a little excitement.

After ordering the special, the trucker called the waiter over again and asked, 'Hey, can you tell me where a guy might find a little pussy around here? I've been on the road for two weeks and haven't had any in a long while – I'm really horny.'

'Sorry,' replied the waiter. 'No women around here.'

Discouraged, the trucker finished his meal and went to the games room to play a game of snooker. Half an hour later, he summoned the waiter again.

'Hey, are you sure there aren't any women around here? I'm really in need of a good lay.'

'Well,' said the waiter, 'if you're really desperate, you can fuck old Wong the Chinaman.' He pointed to an old Chinese man sweeping the floor in the backroom.

'Hey,' said the trucker, 'I don't go for that shit, I want some pussy.'

'Up to you,' replied the waiter wandering off.

An hour later, the trucker was about to leave. He grabbed the waiter once more.

'Are you positive there are no women around here?'

'I'm positive,' said the waiter. 'But you can still fuck old Wong the Chinaman if you want to.'

'I told you I don't go for that shit,' grumbled the trucker. He opened the door to leave. Slowly, he turned back to the waiter. 'But if I did want to fuck old Wong the Chinaman, how much would it cost me?'

'Five pounds.'

'Five pounds to fuck a Chinaman?'

'Hell, no,' answered the waiter, 'five pounds is just for me and my brother Bob to hold old Wong down. He doesn't go for that shit, either!'

Two men were working on a dock. One turned to the other and said, 'Did you know there's a homo working in the crew?'

'No,' his friend replied. 'Who is he?'

'I can't tell you that!'

'Oh, come on!'

'You have to kiss me first.'

●

What do you call a woman with her tongue sticking out?

A lesbian with a hard-on.

●

What do you call a gay Red Indian?

A brave fucker.

●

Did you hear about the gay pope?

He couldn't decide if he was divine or just gorgeous.

●

Did you know that 30 per cent of the gays in Britain were born that way? The other 70 per cent were sucked into it.

●

Do you know what the miracle of AIDS is?

It turns fruits into vegetables.

●

Do you know what you call a gay bar without any bar stools?

A fruit stand.

●

What do lesbians need to open up a gay bar?

A licker licence.

•

Have you heard what GAY really stands for?

Got Aids Yet?

•

Four gay men are sitting in a jacuzzi when suddenly they notice a glob of sperm float to the surface. The oldest of the group turns and shrieks, 'All right, which one of you bitches farted?!'

•

How do you quieten a gay baby?

Shove a dummy up its ass.

•

A man went to the doctor's one day complaining that he thought he was gay.
    'What makes you think you're gay?' asked the doctor.
    'Well,' said the man, 'my grandfather was gay.'
    The doctor explained that he didn't think sexual preference was hereditary.
    'I see,' replied the man, 'but my father was also gay.'
    The doctor said that he thought this was quite unusual, but that this didn't necessarily mean that the man was gay.
    'Okay,' said the man, 'but my brother is gay, too.'
    'My goodness,' exclaimed the doctor, 'doesn't anyone in your family have sex with women?'
    'Oh, yes,' replied the man. 'My sister.'

•

An English officer is assigned to a detachment of American soldiers in a foreign country. The American officer in charge comes over to greet the newcomer.
    'Officer Hayes,' the American says, 'you're going to like it here in our camp. I mean we just don't sit around and watch the grass grow while waiting for orders. Take

Monday nights. On Monday night we all get riproaring drunk.'

'Well that leaves me out,' says the Englishman stiffly, 'I don't drink.'

'Well,' continues the American, 'on Tuesday night we all get wrecked on weed.'

'Sorry,' says the Englishman, 'I don't do that either.'

'Not to worry because on Wednesday we really have a ball, and bring in the chicks from the nearby village. That's when all the real fun begins.'

'Well, I hate to disappoint you, old chap, but I don't go around with cheap women,' the Englishman says flatly.

'Don't go around with cheap women? You're not one of those queers are you?'

Highly insulted, the Englishman says, 'Of course not!'

The American whistles through his teeth and says, 'Well for sure you're not going to like Thursday night!'

●

Have you heard about the gay sperm whale?

He bit the head off a submarine and ate the seamen.

●

What do you call a gay midget?

Sweet and low.

●

What did one lesbian say to the other at the gay bar?

'Care to come back to my place for some twat-tails?'

●

# More Racial Mixtures

What's the difference between an elephant and an Italian grandmother?

Twenty pounds and a black dress.

●

What does eating pussy and being a member of the Mafia have in common?

One slip of the tongue and you're in deep shit.

●

Maria is sitting on her stoop eating a slice of pizza. Two of her girl friends walk by, and notice that she's not wearing any underwear.

'Hey, Maria,' one of them calls, 'did you take off your panties to keep yourself cool?'

'I don't know about keeping cool,' Maria replies, 'but it sure keeps the flies away from my pizza!'

●

How do you kill an Italian?

Smash the toilet seat over his head while he's getting a drink of water.

●

Why don't Italians eat fleas?

Because they can't get their little legs apart.

●

Why does the new Italian navy use glassbottomed boats?

So they can steer clear of the old Italian navy.

●

How can you tell an Italian plane out on the runway?

It's the one with hair under its wings.

●

Three doctors were sitting around drinking coffee one morning after doing early operations.

'Boy,' said the first doctor. 'The operation I performed this morning was the easiest ever.'

'Bet mine was easier,' said the second doctor.

'I'm *sure* mine was the easiest,' said the third.

'I don't know about that,' said the first doctor. 'I operated on a German today.'

'I operated on a Chinaman.'

'I operated on an Italian.'

'Germans have got to be the easiest,' said the first doctor. 'You open them up and they have wheels and gears inside. You simply change a wheel or gear and close.'

The second doctor said, 'You're wrong. The Chinese are the easiest to operate on. They have colour-coded transistors; just change a defective transistor, and you're done.'

'You're both wrong – Italians are by far the easiest to operate on. They only have two moving parts – the mouth and the asshole – and they're interchangeable!'

●

What is an Italian virgin?

A girl who can run faster than her brother!

●

Dracula goes to Rome and checks into the Grand Italia Hotel. The bell-hop, after bringing in his coffin, asks if there is anything else he can do for him. Dracula says, 'Yes there is,' and lunges for the boy's throat.

After draining the blood from him, Dracula throws the bell-hop's lifeless body out of his bedroom window. The body lands on a policeman stationed in front of the hotel. The impact sends the policeman sprawling to the ground.

Meanwhile Dracula still has not satisfied his blood lust, so he goes into the hotel's hallway and grabs a chamber-maid. When finished with her he throws her drained body out the same window.

This body too lands on the unfortunate policeman who had just managed to dust himself off after the first assault. This time, though, he is knocked cold. A half hour later the police commissioner arrives on the scene and manages to get the unconscious officer back to his senses.

'Officer Vetillo, can you explain what is going on here?' the commissioner asks as he looks at the dead drained bodies on the ground.

'I don't honestly know, sir. All I know is that drained wops keep falling on my head.'

●

Did you hear about the new Italian tanks?

They have one speed forward and four in reverse.

●

A Mafia Don, after checking his books realizes there is a thief among his family. The Don calls in his most trusted aide, his first lieutenant, Dominick.

'Dominick, find out who the thief is and bring him to me.'

The next day the lieutenant, Dominick, informs the Don that the thief has been uncovered.

'I am saddened to tell you, Don, that the thief is Nunzio, the deaf-mute.'

Astonished but furious the Don has the lieutenant bring the old deaf-mute before him. But since Nunzio can only communicate by means of sign language, Dominick must act as translator.

'Ask him where he has put the money, Dominick.'

Using sign language, Dominick translates to the wide-eyed and frightened old man. The old man answers that he knows nothing about any money. Nodding, Dominick tells the Don this.

Angered, the Don takes a gun from his desk and places it to Nunzio's now sweating brow. In a threatening voice he tells Dominick to tell the deaf-mute that unless he comes clean, he's going to blow his brains out.

After Dominick finishes translating, Nunzio panics. Realizing the Don is a ruthless killer, Nunzio confesses to Dominick. With fingers flying, Nunzio says, 'Please, don't kill me. The money is in a green garbage bag in my cellar. A thousand pardons, Don!'

When Dominick doesn't translate immediately, the Don questions his lieutenant for an answer.

Without further hesitation Dominick turns to the Don and says, 'He says you don't have the balls to shoot him.'

●

An Italian couple are spending their wedding night at the house of the bride's parents. Rosa sits on the bed as her husband undresses. He takes off his shirt and she sees the thick hair covering his chest. Terribly upset, she runs downstairs to her mother.

'Mama,' she screams. 'He's got hair all over his chest like an animal!'

'Calm down,' her mother says, 'and go back upstairs. It's your wifely duty.'

Up she goes, just in time to see her husband remove his trousers. Again the bride bolts from the room and runs to her mother.

'Mama, he's got hair all over his legs like a monkey!'

'Silly girl, go back upstairs and make love to your husband like a good Italian wife.'

Once again she returns to the bedroom to find her husband removing his shoes, and he has only half of a foot on his left leg.

She runs downstairs and gasps, 'Mama, he has a foot and a half!'

Her mother pushes her aside. 'Stupid girl! You stay down here and *I'll* go upstairs!'

●

Mr. O'Reilly had a terrible problem – he hadn't had a bowel movement in two weeks. When he explained the situation to his doctor, the doctor gave him a box of suppositories and told him to use them all and come back in a week.

Unfortunately, Mr. O'Reilly had never used suppositories before; he supposed they were simply very large pills. So he ate two the first day, four the next, and so on until the box was finished and the week was up.

He returned to the doctor and said, 'Doctor, I did what you told me and I still have no relief.'

The doctor was amazed. 'I don't understand! You've used a whole box of these and you still haven't gone? What have you been doing, eating them?'

'What do you think I've been doing? Shoving them up my ass?'

●

What did the Irish woman say to her unmarried pregnant daughter?

Don't worry, maybe it's not yours.

●

Have you heard about the Irish parachute?

It opens on impact.

●

What do you call an Irishman in a tree?

A branch manager.

Did you hear about the Irishman who thought Moby Dick was a venereal disease?

•

Why don't they have ice cubes in Ireland?

They lost the recipe.

•

Why do Irish men make such lousy lovers?

Because they always wait for the swelling to go down.

•

Did you hear what happened to the Irish dog?

The tree pissed on him.

•

Did you hear about the Irish gardener who broke his arm while he was raking leaves?

He fell out of the tree.

•

The first day of school the new teacher says to her class, 'All right children, I want you to know that I have a very difficult name and I'm going to spell it out for you on the blackboard. Tomorrow if any of you can remember how to spell it right, you'll each get a bag of sweets.' The teacher turns to the board and writes, 'MY NAME IS MISS PRUSSY.'

Little Paddy, who is just over from Ireland, really wants to do well in his new school, so that night he goes home repeating over and over, 'Prussy, Miss Prussy.'

Paddy's older brother hears him and asks him what he's doing. Paddy explains, and his brother says with a grin, 'That's easy to remember. Just think of pussy with an 'r'.

The next day in class, Paddy is anxiously waiting to be called on. He has practised all night and is ready to impress his teacher and his friends. The teacher looks out into the class and spots Paddy looking confident.

'Okay, Paddy, do you remember what my name is?'

In a sudden panic, Paddy tries to think of what his brother told him, and stutters, 'It's a, a, um, Miss CRUNT!'

●

How do you confuse an Irishman?

Put him in a round room and tell him to piss in the corner.

●

Do you know what happened to the Irishman when he picked his nose?

His brains caved in.

●

A nun went to her Mother Superior to complain about the language of the construction workers who were working next to the convent. Sister Margaret was Irish, so the Mother Superior was used to simplifying things for her.

'Sister Margaret, don't get so upset. Those men are just people of the earth. They call a spade a spade,' Mother Superior explained patiently.

Still agitated, Sister Margaret replied, 'Oh no they don't Mother. They call it a fucking shovel!'

●

Why did the Irish lift operator lose his job?

He kept forgetting the route.

●

Why did the Irishman go through the car-wash a second time?

He liked the special effects but he couldn't understand the ending.

●

Did you hear about the Irish college student?

He stayed up all night to study for a urine test – and failed.

●

Why are there so many virgins in Ireland?

Because all the pricks are over here.

●

What's long, white and useless on a woman?

An Irishman.

●

What happens to a Red Indian who drinks too much tea?

He drowns in his tee pee.

●

A Jew, a Protestant and a Catholic died and were waiting at the Pearly Gates. St. Peter came out to interview them.

'You!' he said to the Jew. 'You liked money so much you called your wife 'Penny'. To Hell with you!'

The Protestant stepped up. 'And you!' St. Peter bellowed. 'You liked liquor so much you called your wife 'Sherry'. To Hell with you!'

'Wait a minute,' he called to the Catholic. 'Why are you following them.'

'I don't stand a chance,' the Catholic explained. 'My wife's name is Fanny.'

●

Do you know what makes a man a gentleman in Greece?

He's a man who takes a girl out at least five times before he propositions her younger brother.

●

Three black women are discussing their men.

'I call my man "9",' says the first woman, "cause he's 9 inches long and does it nine times a night.'

'I call my man "10",' says the second woman, "cause he's 10 inches long and does it ten times a night.'

'I call my man "Crême de Menthe",' says the third woman.

'What?' asks the first woman. 'Ain't that a liqueur?'

'Yeh,' replies the third woman, 'yeh, yeh, oh yeh.'

●

A car full of white Southern boys was speeding through a small Georgia town, when they passed a parked sheriff's car. A chase ensued, during which the white boys' car crashed into the back of a car full of blacks who had stopped for a red light. The sheriff arrived at the scene and got out of his car. He walked over to the white boys and said, 'All right boys, how fast were those coons going when they backed up into you?'

●

A teacher stands before her first-grade class one day during a spelling lesson. 'Can anyone here tell me how to spell the word 'before' and use it in a sentence?'

A little redheaded girl is chosen and she says, 'Before, B-E-E.'

'No, I'm sorry, that's incorrect,' says the teacher.

A little blond boy is then called on and he gives it a try. 'Before, B-E-F-O-U...'

'Sorry,' interrupts the teacher, 'that's also incorrect.'

Finally, Tyrone is called on. He is the only black child in the class.

'Before, B-E-F-O-R-E, Before.' says Tyrone looking pleased with himself.

'Very good, Tyrone. Now please use the word 'before' in a sentence.'

After a few minutes of thought, Tyrone says confidently, '2 and 2 be 4!'

●

A young black couple, out on their first date, are sitting under a tree in a neighbourhood park.

'Oh, David, you have such big biceps!' Yolanda says.

'Not really, they measure 20 inches on the tape,' he says.

'Wow,' replies Yolanda, 'how about your chest?'

'I think the last time I measured it, it was 50 inches on the tape.'

'Gee, that's big, but how about your, er, well, er, you know . . .'

Surprised, David says, 'You mean my prick? Why that's two inches.'

'Two inches?!' exclaims Yolanda, 'You mean on the tape?'

'No, I mean two inches from the floor.'

●

Moses is up on Mount Sinai and he suddenly becomes very upset. With his face upturned to the heavens he says in disbelief, 'Now let me get this straight, we're the chosen people and you want us to cut off the tips of our whats?!'

●

A Jewish prospector, down on his luck went into town looking for sex. All the girls in the area wanted 50 bucks and he had only 20.

A madam at one house told him that for 20 dollars she knew a black hooker who might be interested. If that hooker wouldn't take care of him, the madam said, he should come back and she would take him on herself. Half an hour goes by and the Jewish man is back to take up her offer.

Years go by and the old Jew never forgets the madam. One day the Jew is in the same area where he had met the madam and so he goes to her 'house'. When she answers the door she recognizes him right away. They sit and talk for a little, and finally the madam says she has someone she'd like the old Jew to meet.

She calls in a young man about 20 years old and says 'David I'd like you to meet your father.'

The boy looks at the prospector and says, 'Do you mean to tell me I'm half Jewish?!'

Insulted, the old Jew says, 'You ungrateful son of a bitch, if I had had another 30 bucks you'd be half black too!'

•

A Polish girl goes to the gynaecologist. She gets up on the table and spreads her legs. The doctor looks her over and can't believe how badly she has taken care of herself.

'When was the last time you had a check-up?' the doctor asks.

Embarrassed, the Polish girl replies, 'I haven't had any Czechs, but I've had a few Hungarians.'

•

# A LITTLE ZIT ON THE SIDE

## Jasper Carrott

He's been a delivery boy (the terror of Solihull), a toothpaste salesman (for four hours), a folkie (repertoire – two songs) – and the most unlikely and original comic superstar for years.

Now Jasper Carrott reveals more of the outrageous talent that has taken him from the Boggery to a series of one-man shows that won him ITV's Personality of the Year Award.

Discover the do-it-yourself man, how to become star of Top of the Pops and the Carrott guide to dog-training. Relive the simple pleasures of The Magic Roundabout, Funky Moped and the Mole.

# THE DIETER'S GUIDE TO WEIGHT LOSS DURING SEX

## Richard Smith

Tired? Listless? Overweight? Open this book at any page and discover everything you wanted to know about sex, food and dieting but never dreamt of asking.

| Activity | Calories burned |
|---|---|
| *REMOVING CLOTHES* | |
| With partner's consent | 12 |
| Without partner's consent | 187 |
| Unhooking bra | |
|    Using two calm hands | 7 |
|    Using one trembling hand | 96 |
| | |
| *EMBARRASSMENT* | |
| Large juice stain on shorts | 10 |
| | |
| *ORGASM* | |
| Real | 27 |
| Faked | 160 |

(Continued on page 81)

# GULLIBLE'S TRAVELS

## Billy Connolly

He has travelled from the majestic deserts of Doha (twin town of Drumchapel in Scotland) and the teeming markets of Bletchley to the splendour of the Sydney surf and the exotic decadence of the Crawley Leisure Centre.

And here it is — a unique guide to the world, travel, life, death and camel-smells, as seen through the eyes of

'the gangling Glaswegian doyen of bad taste' *Daily Telegraph*

'the man who makes Bette Midler look like Jess Conrad' *The Stage*

'one of the most outrageous Scotsmen ever to have vaulted Hadrian's Wall' *Daily Express*

'the laughing laureate of the loo' *The Times*

the inimitable (thank God) BILLY CONNOLLY

Compiled by Duncan Campbell

Illustrated by Steve Bell

# WELLIES FROM THE QUEEN

## Colin Douglas

Dr David Campbell is all at sea again – but this time it's official. He's joined Her Majesty's Navy as Medical Officer on board the *Winchester*, a small but busy warship. Sleeping sickness, malaria and those little souvenirs from Gibraltar present no problems to a qualified doctor like himself. But how is he to fulfil his duties as SRO (Sexual Relations Officer), WGO (War Graves Officer) and WSO (Whale-Spotting Officer) when he knows nothing about war graves and considerably less about whales?

As the *Winchester* struggles for cod and country off Iceland and confounds the enemy (and just about everyone else) on the sunny beaches of Banjul, David Campbell battles against the bewildering, chaotic forces of naval logic and officialdom.

*Wellies from the Queen* is one of the funniest books about medical highjinks since *Doctor on the Go*.

# THE ART OF COARSE SEX

## Michael Green

Undaunted by the advice of romantic novelists, sex therapists or agony aunts, Michael Green thrusts onwards into the hitherto virgin territory of THE ART OF COARSE SEX. The dismal difficulties of outdoor sex, the ghastly complexities and consequences of furtive affairs, the mysteries of sexual attraction – all this and more is ruthlessly, wickedly and hilariously exposed as Michael Green gets to the bottom of Man's oldest obsession.

# THE UNLUCKIEST MAN IN THE WORLD
## and similar disasters

## Mike Harding

Born in the picturesque spa of Lower Crumpsall, he spent his early years in the brooding shadow of a cream cracker factory. At the age of seventeen he bought a set of Mongolian bagpipes and joined a rock and roll band. Much of his manhood has been spent waiting for a girl wearing red feathers and a hulu skirt to come into his life. He is the incorrigible, irrepressible and slightly mad Mike Harding.

*The Unluckiest Man in the World* takes us into the world of Mike Harding with an inimitable collection of happy, sad, ridiculous, profound and simply hilarious songs, poems and stories.

# BESTSELLING HUMOUR BOOKS FROM ARROW

All these books are available from your bookshop or news-agent or you can order them direct. Just tick the titles you require and complete the form below.

| | | | |
|---|---|---|---|
| ☐ | THE ASCENT OF RUM DOODLE | W. E. Bowman | £1.75 |
| ☐ | THE COMPLETE NAFF GUIDE | Bryson, Fitzherbert and Legris | £2.50 |
| ☐ | SWEET AND SOUR LABRADOR | Jasper Carrott | £1.50 |
| ☐ | GULLIBLE'S TRAVELS | Billy Connolly | £1.75 |
| ☐ | THE MALADY LINGERS ON | Les Dawson | £1.25 |
| ☐ | A. J. WENTWORTH | H. F. Ellis | £1.60 |
| ☐ | THE CUSTARD STOPS AT HATFIELD | Kenny Everett | £1.75 |
| ☐ | BUREAUCRATS — HOW TO ANNOY THEM | R. T. Fishall | £1.25 |
| ☐ | THE ART OF COARSE RUGBY | Michael Green | £1.75 |
| ☐ | THE ARMCHAIR ANARCHIST'S ALMANAC | Mike Harding | £1.60 |
| ☐ | CHRISTMAS ALREADY? | Gray Jolliffe | £1.25 |
| ☐ | THE JUNKET MAN | Christopher Matthew | £1.75 |
| ☐ | FLASH FILSTRUP | Peter Plant | £1.00 |
| ☐ | A LEG IN THE WIND | Ralph Steadman | £1.75 |
| ☐ | POSITIVELY VETTED | Eddie Straiton | £1.75 |
| ☐ | TALES FROM A LONG ROOM | Peter Tinniswood | £1.75 |

Postage _____

Total _____

---

ARROW BOOKS, BOOKSERVICE BY POST, PO BOX 29, DOUGLAS, ISLE OF MAN, BRITISH ISLES

Please enclose a cheque or postal order made out to Arrow Books Ltd for the amount due including 15p per book for postage and packing both for orders within the UK and for overseas orders.

*Please print clearly*

NAME ............................................................................

ADDRESS ......................................................................

......................................................................................

Whilst every effort is made to keep prices down and to keep popular books in print, Arrow Books cannot guarantee that prices will be the same as those advertised here or that the books will be available.